Your Book of English Country Dancing

The *Your Book* Series

Abbeys · Acting · Aeromodelling · Anglo-Saxon England · Animal Drawing · Aquaria · Archaeology · Astronomy
Ballet · Brasses · Breadmaking · Bridges · Butterflies and Moths
Camping · Canals · The Way a Car Works · Card Games · Chess · Contract Bridge · Corn Dollies · Mediaeval and Tudor Costume · Nineteenth Century Costume · Cricket
Dinghy Sailing
Embroidery · English Country Dancing
Film-making · Fishes · Flower Arranging · Flower Making · Forestry
The Guitar · Gymnastics
Hovercraft
Judo
Kites · Knitted Toys · Knots

Landscape Drawing · Light
Magic · Men in Space · Mental Magic · Modelling · Money · Music
Painting · Paper Folding · Parliament · Party Games · Patchwork · Pet Keeping · Photographing Wild Life · Keeping Ponies · Prehistoric Animals · Prehistoric Britain · Pressed and Dried Flowers · Puppetry
Racing and Sports Cars · The Recorder · Roman Britain
Sea Fishing · The Seashore · Secret Writing · Self-Defence · Shell Collecting · Skating · Soccer · Swimming · Survival Swimming and Life Saving
Table Tennis · Table Tricks · Tall Ships · Television · Tennis · Traction Engines
Watching Wild Life · Woodwork

English Country Dancing

Priscilla and Robert Lobley

FABER AND FABER
London Boston

First published in 1980
by Faber and Faber Limited
3 Queen Square, London WC1N 3AU
Printed in Great Britain by
Lowe & Brydone Limited, Thetford, Norfolk
All rights reserved

British Library Cataloguing in Publication Data

Lobley, Priscilla
Your book of English country dancing.
1. Folk dancing, English – Juvenile literature
I. Title   II. Lobley, Robert
793.3'1942   GV1646.E6

ISBN 0-571-11522-5

Contents

Illustrations

Acknowledgements

The authors are grateful to Mozart Allan for permission to quote the tune of "The Dashing White Sergeant" on page 42–3 from *Allan's Ballroom Companion*, and to the English Folk Dance and Song Society for permission to quote the tunes which appear on pages 37–41 and 44–48. All These dances are included in the Society's *Community Dances Manuals*.

Illustrations Nos. 3 and 6 are provided by the Mansell Collection, No. 5 by the London Borough of Southwark, South London Art Gallery, No. 7 by the Mary Evans Picture Library, and Nos. 27 and 29 by Ian Anderson. No. 1 and "A Fiddler and a Hornpipe Dancer" on the title page appear in *Catchpenny Prints*, published by Dover Publications, New York.

Special thanks to Brian, Ben, Jonathan, Kelly, John and Janet for being "The Old Mole" and to Adam and Mary for all their help.

CHAPTER ONE

The history of the dances

When someone plays rhythmic music most people without thinking tap a foot or move about to it. Dancing, moving to music, is a natural and instinctive activity, and over the centuries it has been developed and used in many ways. Dance has been associated with magic, religion, spectacle, ritual, drama and just plain enjoyment. Very early in the history of civilization people used dance as part of their religious ceremonies and some primitive tribes still do. Even in sophisticated Western countries remnants of religious and ritual dances still exist. The sword dances of Scandinavia, Germany and north-east England, the Morris dance, and the Hobby Horse dances are part of these survivals. Morris dances are performed by six or eight men in two columns, usually wearing bells and dancing with handkerchiefs or sticks. Most of the Morris dances come from the Cotswolds but others are from Lancashire and Cheshire and are performed by dancers in clogs. Very few traditional Morris teams remain but many new teams of either men or women have been formed to perform the dances. This is also true of the sword dances of north-east England, which probably owe something to the Vikings. Sword dancers link the swords to form a pattern or lock and in some dances a man enacts a ritual beheading. Two Hobby Horse dances survive at Minehead and Padstow and both suggest rituals of great antiquity.

Very few of the ritual dance ceremonies are now performed for religious or magical reasons; they are usually done to entertain and impress the public. Spectacular display and entertainment dances have a long history, ranging from eccentric and acrobatic dances at medieval fairs to the Royal Ballet. Watching others dance has always been, and remains, a popular occupation; television has provided new opportunities.

1 "The Dog Teaching the Cat to Dance" from an eighteenth-century chapbook.

Although ceremonial and spectacle dances call for selected and trained dancers, ordinary people have always danced for their own enjoyment. At most special occasions there is dancing. If you look at old paintings or prints or photographs you will often see people at weddings, fairs and feasts dancing in the street. At medieval feasts people took hands and sang together, and as they sang they moved in long rhythmic lines – they needed no instruments. As they moved sideways the leader would weave in and out of the throng. This dance was known as a carol and nowadays the dancing has been dropped and just the singing remains. Nevertheless, at crowded festive occasions this natural tendency to form linked lines still remains.

The line dances became circle dances as the two ends joined up, and musical instruments were used instead of the human voice. From the big outdoor feasts the dances moved indoors, and in the process some of the circles became squares or oblongs to fit the room. With the move indoors the upper classes invented rules and conventions for their dances, and danced with style and grace.

2 Dancing in medieval times (taken from a medieval manuscript).

During the reign of Queen Elizabeth the native country dances became firmly established at court. Elizabeth was a very enthusiastic dancer who encouraged all kinds of dancing. The country dances that were done during her reign often included kissing and may have been the forerunners of some children's party games today. The Puritans were unhappy about what they felt was the general immorality surrounding dancing, a recurring view in the history of dance. During the Commonwealth there was some effort by extremists to ban it altogether, although Oliver Cromwell himself was known to be sympathetic to dancing. John Playford, a printer and publisher in London at that time, produced a book of country dances, *The English Dancing Master* (1650), which preserved the tunes and figures of the dances. Its subsequent editions helped popularize English country dancing in Europe and America. In the eighteenth century the French aristocracy had romantic ideas about the delights of country life, and the country dance, or contredanse as it became known, was very popular. The first part of an evening would be taken up with formal dances, minuets and gavottes, and in the second half everyone would relax and dance the rustic dances.

3 Dancing in the seventeenth century (from an engraving).

4 Frontispiece from *The English Dancing Master* by John Playford.

5 "The Dance" from *The Happy Marriage* by William Hogarth (London Borough of Southwark, South London Art Gallery).

The popularity of the country dance in France kept the English upper classes interested, and until the arrival of the waltz and polka in the nineteenth century it remained an important accomplishment for any young gentleman or lady to know the old and new country dances. During the early years of Queen Victoria's reign the country dance began to lose its popularity amongst the upper classes, as new exciting couple dances swept the ballrooms. Then with the death of Prince Albert the court went into mourning, and much social dancing suffered an eclipse. By the end of the century the only country dance many people knew was "Sir Roger de Coverley", as it was customary to close the evening with it. But the old dances had remained alive in the villages and in America, where dances and songs taken from England by the settlers had remained popular in some remote communities.

6 A detail from *Don Luigi's Ball* by Thomas Rowlandson.

Towards the end of the nineteenth century, with its intensive industrialization and materialism, some people began to feel a romantic nostalgia for a simpler life. Artists and poets withdrew into a world of mock medievalism. Town suburbs with a village atmosphere were conceived and built, and sentimental drawings of children from a bygone age by Kate Greenaway, Walter Crane and Randolph Caldecott became popular. It was only natural that people should start to search for the unspoilt music and dances of the countryfolk. One of the most energetic and thorough of these people was Cecil Sharp, who travelled round the country collecting songs and dances. He published both and found a receptive public keen to dance the old dances and sing the old songs. From the turn of the century there was a tremendous revival of country dancing in various forms. Mary Neal, one of the earliest pioneers, believed that Merrie England with happy folk dancing on the village greens could be re-created, but unfortunately the dream was shattered by the First World War. After the war the revival movement under the influence of Sharp became rather educational and female-dominated, and the happy hedonistic dancers in the towns turned to imported American jazz dance crazes. Fortunately, in some villages and small towns in remote areas the old country dances remained largely unaffected by the revival or by the American dances.

During the Second World War there was a renewed interest in country dance. Paradoxically, one of the reasons for this was the popularity of American square dancing brought over by American troops during the war. The old dances from England and France had gone over to America in the seventeenth

7 *Dancing on the Green* (about 1880).

and eighteenth centuries and returned in a modified form in the 1940s and 50s. With the encouragement of the Queen, or Princess Elizabeth as she then was, square dancing swept the country. As well as in the big dance halls it even became popular in the small villages hitherto fairly unaffected by fashion. When the craze receded it left the traditional country dancers and the revivalists of the English Country Dance Society doing a mixture of English and American dances. Although the popularity of traditional dancing in much of the country slowly dwindled, in some areas it remained strong and in the towns barn dances found a new popularity amongst people who wanted to organize social get-togethers – dances to cater for all ages and to help everyone to get to know each other. These social barn dances continue to be very popular. In recent years there has been a renewed interest in country dance allied to the general enthusiasm for country topics and rural ways, and the popularity of folk rock music has also introduced many young people to folk music and dance in general. This renewed interest has been reflected in the popularity of folk festivals and folk clubs. It has also sent enthusiasts out into the country again, looking for the last remnants of village country dances and old country musicians.

CHAPTER TWO
The music

It is strange to think that a great number of the tunes that we dance to today may be the same as those in popular use two hundred years ago or more. The attraction of the melodies is such that they have been lovingly handed down from generation to generation of musicians, mostly learnt by ear and remembered through a lifetime of playing. Many dance tunes were freely adapted from popular songs and this may explain the way they have travelled round the country, some tunes occurring all over the British Isles, which is extraordinary considering the limitation of communications until the present times. A tune recorded by Jim Cameron's Scottish band in the 1940s is exactly the same as one written down in the Thomas Hardy family tune book that dates from the early nineteenth century. Dances, songs and their tunes have been written down and published in various ways in the past three centuries and in some forms have been obtainable by working people as well as the gentry.

8 An Oxfordshire Village Band.

From the nineteenth century popular music-making has undergone numerous changes, particularly in England. In the middle of the nineteenth century the introduction of harmoniums and organs into the churches and chapels led to the breaking up of many a village band who had formerly played for the services and who, without the financial support from church funds, were unable to buy and keep up their instruments, mainly fiddles, cellos etc. On the other hand, the production of cheap concertinas and melodeons later in the century gave many musicians with limited means the chance to acquire instruments superbly suited to playing traditional music. In this century other influences have made themselves felt: the popularity of the brass bands, especially in the cities, and jazz, perhaps the greatest craze of all, which came at a time when recordings and wireless were able to popularize it world-wide.

In quieter rural areas of the British Isles, which have been more reluctant to change old ways, there is still music-making in the old style to be found. In the Shetlands, the north-east, East Anglia, most of Scotland and Ireland, for instance, amongst certain families, in particular pubs, traditional playing can still be heard and much of the style of our present country-dance bands comes from such sources.

English traditional dance music has four different rhythms, each one giving a tune its pace and individuality. These are:

The Reel or March
The Jig
The Polka or Hornpipe
The Waltz

To the dancer who does not play music the differences are very subtle, and, apart from the waltz and sometimes the polka, they will not much affect the way you dance.
In simple non-musical terms:

The *Reel* or *March* has a steady even beat expressed by saying RUM TUM RUM TUM etc.

The *Jig* has a bouncy rhythm expressed by saying HICKORY DICKORY HICKORY DICKORY etc.

The *Polka* or *Hornpipe* has an even more bouncy rhythm expressed by saying ONE POTATO TWO POTATO etc.

The *Waltz* is a slow smooth rhythm expressed by saying ONE TWO THREE ONE TWO THREE etc.

In musical terms:

The Reel

The March

The Jig

The Polka or Hornpipe

The Waltz

Natural rhythmic playing can only be learnt by ear and happily the tape recorder and record player have become the modern, albeit mechanized, substitute for the 'oral tradition' that kept music alive in the past. Musicians and bands also have the opportunity to get together at various folk festivals, and such is the diversity of music-making round the British Isles that there seems little chance of standardization prevailing.

CHAPTER THREE

Dance formation and progression

Certain practical rules apply wherever the dance is held, whether it is a barn, a scout hut or the ballroom of the Town Hall. Usually a hall is rectangular and has a stage at one end. This will be where the band and Master of Ceremonies perform and it is known as the 'Top' end. All the dancers line up from this end, and all the dances start from it. If the room is very elongated in shape it may have a stage at the side for the band and M.C. Then for certain longways dances which need the length, the Caller will have to declare one end of the room the 'Top' end. Otherwise dancers will line up to the band on the stage as the 'Top', in the usual way.

Occasionally big dances may have both an M.C. and a Caller for the evening, but for most events the two jobs are rolled into one. The M.C.'s task is to make sure that the evening's programme runs smoothly and that everybody enjoys themselves. The Caller must teach the dances to everyone and then help them through by clever prompting. Not easy work for two people, and even harder for one. The success of the evening depends a lot on both the personality and the skill of the M.C. and the Caller, and even experienced ones can have bad moments.

When enough people have arrived the Caller will announce the name of the first dance, and will also say how many dancers he needs for each group in the dance. This is called the 'Set' in country dancing.

Before all else you will need to find yourself a partner. However much people try to change tradition it is still usual for the men to ask the girls to dance, unless they are friends or know each other quite well. If you are very shy by nature try to overcome it. Nobody minds if you don't know the dance, and you will usually find people helping you through as much as possible. (Everyone has been a beginner once.) It is a good idea at first to seek out the dancers who look as if they know what they are doing, because they can give you a lot of confidence at the start. If you are a girl and have decided that you don't want to join the dance that is being started, don't stand or sit close to where the action is. It is embarrassing for men to have polite requests to dance turned down and it wastes their time in finding a partner. It would be ideal if everyone just got up and danced with anyone close to hand, but if country dances are not quite as friendly as that, at least they are a step in the right direction.

The Formation of the Set

Now to come back to the Set. There are three main groupings: the Longways Set, the Square Set and the Circle Set.

The Longways Set. A nice easy way of setting up a dance. Just face your partner. He should have his LEFT shoulder to the band and Caller, she should have her RIGHT shoulder likewise. So all the men should have formed into a line facing all the girls in a line. Some longways dances are for 'as many as will', others may be for anything between three and six couples. Just listen to the Caller.

The Square Set. Four couples only are involved for this one. Be sure that the men are standing on the girls' left. One couple stands with their backs to the band (they are called the Top Couple), two couples stand on either side and one couple faces the Top Couple – in a square!

9 The Square Set.

The Circle Set. Couples join hands in a big circle right round the room, man on girl's left. This is called a Grand Circle; a variation of it is the Sicilian Circle, in which couple faces couple in a big circle round the room. In the Double Sicilian Circle two couples face two couples in a large circle if space allows. But as there is rarely room for this, it is possible to do the dances that need this formation in a long line, with the progression taking place in the same way as in a longways dance.

10 The Double Sicilian Circle.

Couple Dances

From the nineteenth century onwards it became admissible and fashionable for men and women to face each other and dance very close together with arms around each other for the whole duration of the dance – just as a couple. Group dances have never been quite the same since. Hundreds of interesting dances for two have been invented since the waltz and the polka swept the ballroom, and some of them gained popularity in the country districts, where they became incorporated into the village hop repertoire, giving variety to an evening of the older traditional dances. There are signs that the same inclination is coming back and you may find one or two couple dances included in the evening's programme.

Progression

This is a fundamental ingredient, and means that sometimes you and your partner move around the set (or up and down it) to meet other dancers. Sometimes you do this on your own in certain square and circle dances. Although progression should be described as a figure (see p. 31), we have mentioned it in this chapter as it is best to know about it when you are forming into sets. It nearly always happens and it is part of the interest in country dancing. However, it is the part that unnerves and confuses you most when you are a beginner. One always thinks, if only I could stay put I might get the hang of this. In a dance that is composed mostly of beginners the Caller, realizing the difficulty, will quite often limit the progressive dances. Nevertheless, you have to learn as quickly as possible what is going on and it is nothing like so worrying once you know what you should be doing.

If a Longways Set dance is limited in length to three to six couples then the progression is reasonably simple. Usually what happens is this: the couple which is at the top of the set at a given point in the dance goes down to the bottom, staying there whilst all the other couples move up. The dance continues the number of times that there are couples in the set, each couple going to the bottom of the set when they reach the top until everyone finally returns to their original position.

The progression which is far the most tricky is in the Longways Set for as many as will (often this stretches right down to the bottom of the hall). The correct dance term for this set is Duple-Minor, so named because the figures are danced by groups of two couples within the whole Set. Every alternate couple from the top of the set is called a Top Couple. This is made easier for everyone to work out by firstly making circles of four from the Top. Now throughout the dance, at a certain point, the Top Couples will move down the set and the couples in between will change places with them to move up to the Top. This means that if you are a Top Couple you move down to the bottom of the set, one couple at a time. Other couples move up to the top. When you arrive at either end you stop dancing whilst the dance goes through once. You then join the set again, because a couple will now be free to dance with you. You then dance back in the opposite direction, and must remember that you have also reversed your role as Top or Bottom Couple.

These instructions should give you a rough idea of the progression in most popular longways dances. When you become more experienced you will find that there are some dances that require alternate men and girls down the line. They are difficult for the beginner, so we will not confuse you at this stage – it could put you off. But you may like to know that they are called 'Improper'!

Progression in the Square Set is much easier. The 1st (or Top) couple lead the dance through. Then the 2nd, 3rd and 4th follow suit, everyone staying in their own positions. The other alternative that occurs, especially in American Squares, is that only the girls move on round the set, dancing with each man in turn until they get back to their own partner.

In the Grand Circle it is usually the men only who move on round the ring, dancing with each girl in turn when the Caller gives the reminder.

In the Sicilian Circle formation a simple change is usually done by passing the opposite couple and dancing on to meet the next.

Changing places and meeting other dancers is one of the real pleasures in country dancing and gives it spontaneous friendliness. You will soon pick up the technique as you go along.

CHAPTER FOUR

Steps, figures and how to to do them

The Steps

There are no very complicated steps in English country dancing. The typical step is simply a jaunty walk or amble in time to the music. There are some regional variations, some opportunity for free expression, but the main interest is in the figures and progressive movements. In earlier times traditional footwear may have influenced the style of stepping, and in areas and amongst classes where heavy footwear was worn a more vigorous footwork was possibly employed, with hop stepping and occasional stamping steps. There is no pointing of the toe as in Scottish country dancing and no jumping or springing steps to contend with. The only variations on the 'jaunty walk' step are a hop step, the rant or polka step and the waltz step. Although the simple walking step has been advocated in the teaching of country dancing for a long time, there has recently been increased interest in a slower pace of dance that requires a more pronounced stepping, and if dancing comes quite naturally and easily to you, then you will find this more fun and interesting to do. On the other hand your proficiency in stepping is in no way vital. The only important thing is to listen to the music and to move the whole body in time to it.

In dance music the beat or rhythm is of first importance and the tune keeps it going. The right sound immediately makes you feel like getting up and jigging about. For most dances all you need to do is the basic walking step, with a slight hop if you are sure of the rhythm and timing of the music. There are also two more basic steps which you will need when the music has a polka or waltz rhythm (see chapter 2).

Hornpipe or Polka: the one, two, three and hop step. Take a firm step to your left, down with your right foot, down with your left and hop on it. Then do the same to the right. The polka is a very springy step on the balls of the feet without the heels touching the ground. Hum something like 'Little Brown Jug' and try it out on your own, so that you practise the one, two, three, hop step in time to polka music, which has a distinct bouncy rhythm. When you have got the hang of it, practise dancing round in circles and then practise with a partner.

The Waltz. The country waltz step and the ballroom waltz step are different and it is useful to learn how to do both. In the country waltz you progress forward with a curving movement first to the right and then to the left. Sway your body to the right, putting your right foot down, then a small dab of a step across with your left, and then back on your right. Do the same swaying movement to the left. When you do this with your partner take inside hands, sway away from each other, then back. The music is not slow, so you will find time for only one strong beat and two very small ones for each sway.

The ballroom waltz step is a little harder to tackle if you have never done any ballroom dancing. The pace of the music should be very slow and measured – 3 even beats to the bar. Take a step forward with your right foot, a step to the side with the left, and feet together with the right. Then go forward with the left foot, a step to the side with the right and feet together with the left. Practise counting one, two, three as you go and if you are female you've got to go backwards! When you are happy with the steps try raising the body to make yourself taller for a second as you move to the side. This could add the graceful up-and-down elegance of the ballroom to your waltzing!

When you can do this easily, practise going round in circles and then try it with a partner. 'Daisy Daisy' is a good easy tune to hum as you go.

In addition to these basic dancing steps there are four other steps that you will need to know.

The side-step. Do just what it says. Take a step to the side and feet together. Then repeat. When this is done slowly it is called the 'chassé' step and when it is fast it is called the 'gallop' step.

The balance. The balance step sometimes but not always precedes the swing. It is a courtesy movement that has its origin in the bow and curtsey. Take a step with a hop to the right, lightly step down with your left foot, and then almost immediately put your weight back on to your right foot. Repeat this stepping to the left, and that completes the balance movement. It can be varied a good deal with vigorous capers when you become more experienced, and have had the opportunity to watch other dancers. Your arms should naturally swing with your body, first to the right and then to the left. Often you will find that there is time to do the balance movement twice.

The swing. The swing is your opportunity in country dancing to get close to your partner, so make the most of it. Do NOT clasp hands across in nursery-school fashion. It looks silly and takes too much room on the dance-floor. Get together in a ballroom hold (man's left hand in girl's right hand, man's right arm round girl so that the hand rests beneath her shoulder-blades, and girl's left arm resting on her partner's shoulder. Extend clasped hands out but keep elbows slightly bent.) The man controls the momentum of the swing with the arm that is round his partner's back.

The step you use for the swing can be one of two.

11 The Swing.

(1) A simple walking step which is easy to do and can have quite a bit of go in it. The dancers face each other to walk round in a clockwise circle with their right feet close together. Lean slightly back from your partner at shoulder level and put some bounce into the step as you go round.

(2) The pivot step gives extra speed and fun. It is a bit like travelling by scooter on the spot, if anyone can remember that nowadays! The hand and feet positions are the same as the walk swing. Use your right (inside) foot as the pivot to hop up and down on, and your left (outside) foot to push along with.

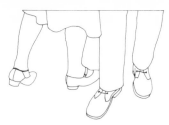

12 Walking step for Swing.

This applies to both dancers. Your feet don't take you anywhere, you just pivot round in a circle – fast! Most important is to get a good bouncy rhythm going. Your right pivoting foot comes down on the beat every time, and your left foot quickly pushes along in the gaps (the off-beat). The swing is difficult to explain in words, and no two people dance it in quite the same way. Watch other dancers who can do it with style and feeling and learn from them.

The rant step. The main distinction of this step is its rhythm and that's not possible to explain in words. It is a kind of stepping that may be varied to suit individual taste, and has always remained popular in the north of England, where it is done in the north-west processional Morris dances as well as the traditional country dances. In country dancing it is usually danced to the rhythm of a reel played at a good measured pace, such as 'Morpeth Rant' or 'Soldier's Joy'.

Take a step and hop on to your left foot, and as you land on it from the hop tap your right foot across, with the ball of the foot lightly stamping the ground (this takes half a bar of music). Then step hop back on to your right foot and pause (this takes the other half bar of music). Then repeat the hopping on your right foot with the left foot tapping across. This description can give only a vague indication of the rant step. If possible find someone to show it to you. You will find it great fun to do.

The Figures

So now you know what to do with your feet. Next you must know where they are going to take you, and these movements and changes of direction in dancing are called figures. There are seven extremely easy and basic ones that occur all the time and you will find them no trouble at all. There are nine more that are a little harder and will require practice in order to do them with confidence. Once you have discovered how to do them you will find that all the usual and popular English country dances are permutations of them. The important thing, once you know them, is, first, to hear and remember the order in which you will be doing them in the dance which the Caller is teaching you. Secondly, and vital if the dance is to go well, you must help through the dance any dancers in your set who are less familiar with the figures than you. That way everybody enjoys the evening.

Here are the sixteen figures – easy ones first. Listen to the music, and when it goes – *you* go.

13 Circle left and right.

1) CIRCLE LEFT AND RIGHT Join hands with your partner and the dancer beside you and side step to the left until the music reaches halfway, then side step back again to where you started. (When this is done with two couples only in a circle it is sometimes called Hands Four.)

2) FORWARD AND BACK (or Advance and Retire, or In and Out in circle dances). Everyone takes hands in line, about shoulder level, and walks or hop steps four beats of music forward and four back. You do this as the music dictates (the Caller will prompt you too), putting a bounce into the movement as you start to move backwards. Sometimes you will do a forward and back twice to a line of music. Sometimes you will forward and back once, followed by forward and cross over.

14 Right and left hand turn. (See page 30.)

29

3) RIGHT AND LEFT HAND TURN Take right hands with the dancer opposite, circle round and return to place. Take left hands, circle round and return to place.

15 Right hand star.

4) RIGHT AND LEFT HAND STAR Facing opposite couple, girls move forward and join right hands; men join right hands above to make the star and then walk round to the left. Change to left hands and circle star back to place.

5) LEAD DOWN TO FORM ARCH AT BOTTOM OF SET The Top Couple lead the dancers down to the bottom, the men in a line going left at the top, the girls in a line going right at the top. When the Top Couple meet at the bottom they join hands to make an arch and the other couples go through it to re-form the set.

16 Promenade. 17 Back to back.

6) PROMENADE This just means walking side by side with your partner, either up or down the set if it is longways, or round in an anti-clockwise direction if it is a square or circle dance. You can simply hold hands together, left hands clasped on top of right hands, or you can leave the right hands free to rest on girl's shoulder or waist.

7) BACK TO BACK (the American name of Do-Si-Do is also frequently used). Just as the name implies, you face the dancer opposite you and back round each other, moving forwards and then backwards without turning the body round. When moving forwards pass by with your right shoulders and when moving back to place pass by with left shoul-

ders (Right Back to Back). In most dances Right Back to Back is followed by Left Back to Back, in which you move forward and pass by left shoulders, moving back to place by passing by right shoulders.

8) CASTING This is the name given to the progressive movement in longways dances. It is a pleasant curving movement which enables a couple to change places with the couple below them in the set. When it is your turn to 'cast', simply face up to the top of the set with your partner, and then turn outwards in a semi-circle round and behind the dancer below you in the set, who simultaneously moves up into the place you have left, as you move into his or her place.

9) THE HEY (or Figure of Eight or Reel of Three). This is an intertwining movement between three dancers in a line. Think of the shape of the number 8 as the pattern you are making as you dance. The person who is starting the Hey (No. 1) faces down and the two others (Nos. 2 and 3) face up the line. No. 1 passes No. 2 with right shoulders and then passes No. 3 with left shoulders. Just remember to alternate right shoulder with left, left shoulder with right until you come back to place.

10) GRAND CHAIN This is the same intertwining movement as the Hey but with all the dancers in one big circle. It always starts with facing your partner and taking right hands. The men then all move on round the circle in an anti-clockwise direction and the girls in a clockwise one. After right hands with your partner you take left hands with the next and then right etc., weaving round the whole circle. In American Squares you sometimes grand chain halfway and then grand chain back to place. Remember if you are the man you should be meeting girls only and vice versa. Unfortunately this simple rule goes astray when two women are dancing together.

18 Grand Chain progression.

31

11) RIGHT AND LEFT HAND THROUGH A miniature Grand Chain done with two couples only, so that the shape is a square instead of a circle. Each man faces the opposite dancer (who may, or may not, be his partner) in a clockwise direction, and the girls face in an anti-clockwise direction. Pass this person opposite with right shoulders and take left hands as you pass the next (a pleasing variation at this point is to do a left hand turn as in a Ladies' Chain). The continue round, passing right shoulders and then left (with another left turn if you did it before) back to place, which completes the figure.

19 Ladies' Chain.

12) LADIES' CHAIN Although this figure looks complicated when you watch it being done for the first time, it is in fact quite simple, and involves everyone in a pleasant swinging change of partners which is satisfying when you get it right. Couple facing couple, the girls go forward to meet each other and take right hands as they pass by to meet the opposite man. Taking her left hand with his as if to promenade, the man puts his right arm quickly round the girl's waist to guide her round in a speedy anti-clockwise turn. As this is done at a fast pace it is a help if the girl leans slightly back against this supporting arm (if it's there in time!) and places her right hand over the man's hand, which will be resting on her hip. The girls go forward again, taking right hands as they pass by to meet their partners, with whom they repeat the same turning movement as before. That completes the Ladies' Chain and it all fits into eight bars of music. In certain square dances it is sometimes done with all four couples. The four girls meet in the middle and walk a right hand star halfway round, then meet and give left hands to the opposite man as they both turn in an anti-clockwise circle; girls go back to centre and repeat back to place. In American square dancing this is called Ladies Grand Chain.

13) DIP AND DIVE As the name suggests, couples face each other to duck under and over each other's

arches. Make the arch by taking inside hands with your partner and lower and raise it alternately as you meet each couple in the dance. The main difficulty is knowing when you should be making the arch and when you should be ducking underneath. A good rule to remember is that the couple who starts it off (the Top Couple) begin by dipping and thereafter you do the opposite of the couple coming towards you. Once you have started off you must alternate the action for each couple you meet.

20 Dip and Dive.

14) POUSSETTE This is the push-and-pull method for couples to change places in a progressive longways dance. Extend arms with elbows bent. The girls put their hands in the men's upturned hands. Then the men in the Top Couples push their partners forward, move to their right and pull them back to face a new couple. At the same time the men in the other couples pull their partners back, move to their left and push them forward to face a new couple.

15) THE BASKET A swing for two couples. Go forward to meet the other couple in a circle; men put their arms round the girls' waists, girls rest their arms on the men's shoulders. Everyone should keep their right feet close to centre and using the pivot step circle round as fast as they like. 'Shoulders back – bottoms in' is an apt motto to remember.

21 The Basket.

16) STRIP THE WILLOW Men in a line face girls in a line. The Top Couple link right arms and step round on the spot, turning clockwise one and a half times

to face the next in line of the opposite sex. Dance forward to him (or her), link left arms and circle once round anti-clockwise. Return to centre, right arms with your partner again and circle once . . . and back to the next person in line of opposite sex and so on until you reach the bottom of the set.

22 Strip the Willow.

The Style

It is important to know the steps and figures for your own confidence and enjoyment, but this will come surprisingly quickly once you have been to a dance or two. It is difficult to dance in a relaxed enthusiastic way until you have had a bit of practice, but the main advantage of English country dancing is that you do not need the skills of the expert dancer. It is basically a sociable means for people to get together and enjoy themselves. More important than anything else is to have this in mind. It is a chance to lose some energy, even have a rave-up if that's what you want to do.

When you do a right and left hand turn, use it as a form of greeting. Take hands firmly, try the occasional nod, say hallo or even just smile. Every movement implies friendliness, closeness, but with a certain restrained formality. One is always part of a group, and that's what makes the whole occasion satisfying.

CHAPTER FIVE

A selection of dances

Instructions for Dancing (called Dance Notation)

The directions for dancing have to be thought of in relation to the music, and a simple way of explanation used. The musical construction is never of much significance to the non-musician. A tune simply starts, continues and stops. What happens in fact is that most dance-tunes are made up of two eight-bar melody lines and each of these is repeated. The first melody of the dance-tune is often called the A music and the second melody is called the B music. Thus if the A music is repeated it is known as A1 the first time and A2 the second time, and the B music if repeated is called B1 and B2. This is probably more comprehensible to musicians, who will also know that the whole amounts to thirty-two bars of music – the length that many country dances are based on. As so many invaluable dance manuals are notated in this way we've followed suit, but if you can't get the hang of all these A's and B's just think of each section of the dance, which is sixteen steps, as done to one line of the melody.

Occasionally you will find certain dances requiring more music, to make forty bars. The band will play an extra repeat of the B music and this will be called B3. For forty-eight bar dances a third melody may be introduced, and this will be called C music (C1 and C2 if it is repeated).

Here is the notation for ten dances. We have mostly chosen very popular ones, because they are good in themselves and you will probably find more chance of dancing them.

I. Mole's Circle Dance

Music	32-bar jigs or polkas.
Formation	Double circle, men on the inside facing out.
A1	Take hands with your partner and slip step to the men's right and back to the left.
A2	Right arm turn, left arm turn.

B1 Balance right and left (hop on to right foot and swing the left leg across, then hop back on to the left foot and swing the right leg across). Do this twice, and then a two-hand turn.

B2 Promenade (men pass on – progression).

2. Buttered Peas
(*from Yorkshire*)

Music	Set tune or similar steady march tune (hop step when appropriate in the dance).
Formation	Couple face couple (girl on man's right) in a long line down the room, or in a big circle round the room.
A1	Circle left and circle back right.
A2	Right and left hand star, grasping up-turned thumbs.

B1	Partners shake right hands and clap three times, then the same with left hands. Couples polka round and change places.
B2	Two men and two girls shake right hands and clap three times, then same again with left hands. Two men and two girls arm right, and then back with arm left.

37

3. Black Jack

(This popular dance was first published in an eighteenth-century dance book.)

Music	Set tune.
Formation	Couple face couple in a big circle.
A1	Clap hands on first beat and circle round to the left.
A2	Clap hands on first beat and circle back to the right.
B1	Face your partner, clap your hands together, clap right hands with your partner, clap your hands together again and then left hands with your partner. You then both turn and repeat this once more with the other couple.

Girls change places passing by with left shoulders and turn quickly round; men do the same passing by with right shoulders.

Change places back again to where you were . . .

Facing other couple walk past each other, passing right shoulder, on to the next couple.

(The last part of the dance must be done neatly and speedily because there is very little time in the music.)

4. Cumberland Square Eight

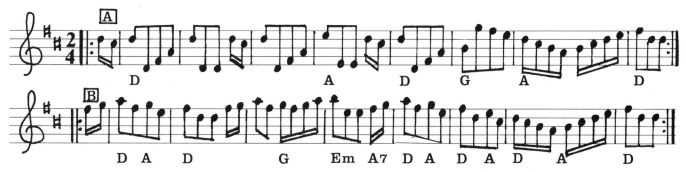

Music	32-bar jigs or reels.
Formation	Square set for 4 couples.
A1	Top Couples gallop across the set (with 4 bars of music you can go a long way) and gallop back to place.
A2	Side Couples do the same.
B1	Top Couples do right hand star and left hands back.
B2	Side Couples do the same.
A3	Top Couples form a basket (see p. 33). and swing.
A4	Side Couples do the same.
B3	All join hands and circle left.
B4	Promenade with partners back to place.

23 Cumberland Square Eight.

39

5. Kendal Ghyll
(from Yorkshire)

40

Music	Set tune.
Formation	Long set for three couples.
A	Join hands in a circle and slip to the left, then back to the right.
B	Men dance a hey (figure of eight) while girls do the same.
C1	Take hands for arches. (Traditionally partners used to link up with knotted handkerchiefs.) First couple under the second and over the third until everyone is back to place.
C2	Repeat C1
D	First couple cast to the bottom of the set followed by second and third couples, men to the left and girls to the right. The first couple make an arch at the bottom of the set and the other couples go under progressing to new places in the set.

Repeat the dance three times for the couples to get back to their original places.

6. The Dashing White Sergeant

(popular in Scotland, but probably originated in England)

Music	Set tune and other 32-bar reels.
Formation	Sicilian circle, three facing three round the room (now usually done with man and two girls on left and right).
A1	Join hands in a circle of six and dance round to the left. Dance back to place.
A2	Each man turns to the girl on his right. Balance step to the right and left, take hands and circle round. Then do the same with the other girl.
B1	Each set of three do a hey (figure of eight) each man facing up to the girl on his right first.
B2	Each set of three take hands and go forward to meet each other, then go back. Go forward again, pass each other by to meet another set of three, and the dance starts again.

7· Nottingham Swing

(Collected in Northamptonshire, by Sibyl Clark)

Music	16-bar hornpipe tunes.
Formation	Longways set for unlimited number of couples. Men, left shoulders to the band, in a line facing girls in a line. From the 'Top' of the room couples take hands with the next couple to make 1st and 2nd couples.
Step	Step-hopping with a bit of a bounce to it.
A (1st half)	1st men and 2nd girls link right arms and circle round twice on the spot.
(2nd half)	1st girls and 2nd men do the same.

B (1st half) 1st couples dance two steps down towards the bottom of the room taking inside hands, change hands and dance back up. Then cast around the 2nd couples (all couples change places as they travel up or down the room).

(2nd half) Swing partners, ready to start the dance again with another couple.

44

8. Circassian Circle

(a favourite finishing dance from Northumberland)

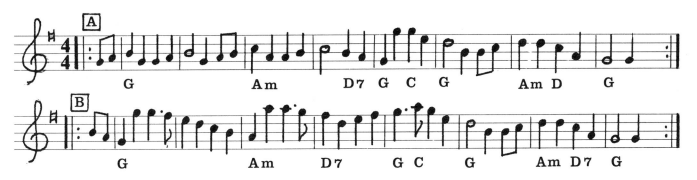

Music	Any selection of rousing 32-bar tunes.
Formation	Grand circle, men standing on the girls' left.
A1	All join hands and stride forward to centre and back. Do this again.
A2	Girls go into centre and clap hands as they move back to place. Men do the same.
B1	Swing with your partner, or polka round.
B2	Promenade.

9. Dorset Four Hand Reel

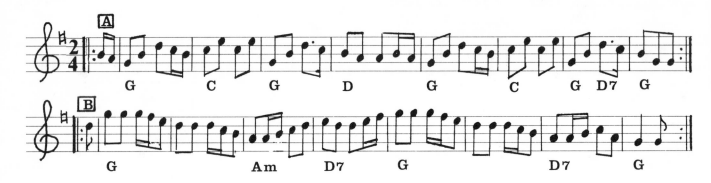

Music	Set tune (there are other variants that may be used).
Formation	Two couples in a line of four. Face partners with the two girls standing back to back.
Steps	A walking step is usual for the first time through the dance, and a lively polka step for the second time through. When partners step to each other a 'show off' rant stepping is most popular.

A1 and A2	Everyone face partners, and passing by with the right shoulders you all dance a continuous hey until you are back to place, with the men facing each other in the centre.
B1	The men step to each other.
B2	They turn to their partners, who join in the stepping.

46

A3 and A4	Repeat the reel nearly twice through so that you are back where you started and the girls face each other. (This time take hands, if you like, to give the dance more movement and excitement.)
B3	The girls step to each other.
B4	They turn to their partners, who join the stepping.

The dance is now usually repeated using a faster polka step and finishes with everybody swinging partners. Warn musicians to play an extra eight bars of B music.

10. Stoke Golding Country Dance

(from Leicestershire, collected by Miss Lambert)

Music Anything that starts fairly fast and ends very fast – slip jigs are ideal.

Formation Long set for 4 or 5 couples.
The top man meets the bottom girl in the set halfway down and they swing, then go back to place.
The bottom man and top girl do the same.
The Top Couple strip the willow down to the bottom of the set (see p. 34).
The top man takes his partner's hand to form an arch and leads her up on the outside of the girls' line and down on the outside of the men.

When they reach the bottom of the set he propels her in to the swing with the new top man as the dance begins again.

(The dance does not have to fit with the music. Couples can swing for as long as they like!)

24 Stoke Golding Country Dance.

CHAPTER SIX

Calling the dances

In England in the past, as in present-day Scotland and Ireland, people arrived at a dance knowing the dances. In England in recent times it has become customary to depend on a Caller for instruction and guidance.

You may find you are asked by friends to show them some dances, or you may decide that you would like to try calling. Either way, be sure you really know the dances first. It is most important that a Caller should appear to be confident at all times, and to be confident you must be prepared.

Write out all the dances you know on pieces of card and try them out with music at home. It may seem silly to dance a whole set by yourself with imaginary people and a gramophone record, but you can try out the calls at just the right moment as you dance. Practise making the calls a moment before the change of figure to give the dancers time. Overcome the tendency to call the moves as you do them.

To be a good Caller you need to be very patient and to give very clear instructions. You also have to be able to build up some sort of rapport with the dancers, as you are responsible for the atmosphere of the whole evening. Don't be surprised at how slow beginners are at understanding your explanations. Never get annoyed – dancing and remembering figures are very difficult for most people. Walk everyone through the dance figure, watch for any groups who look lost and if necessary reshow the moves. If one group has got the hang of it, get them to demonstrate for the others. When you are satisfied that most people know the dance, ask the band to play and call the moves clearly. At first the dancers will need your calls but slowly they will become confident and you can stop calling. Keep an eye on the dance-floor and don't hesitate to start calling again if you see anyone in difficulties. It is quite useful to note one couple at the beginning of the dance and to watch their progress round or up and down the room, so that you know by their position when to stop the dance. Don't forget to give ample warning to the band when you want them to end.

Some Callers use gramophone records for music, and they can be useful for small occasions, but it is much better if possible to use live music. If you have a musician or band find time to discuss the dances you want to do before the dance starts. Never assume that they can just play any tune you want. Sometimes they will want to substitute other tunes. In that case make sure they know whether you want marches, jigs or hornpipes and how many bars of music the dance takes. It is important to get on as well with the band as with the dancers, so be considerate and work as a team.

Before the first dance begins, decide at what time you will have a break. If there are organizers, discuss with them the arrangements for the evening. At a lot of club dances people hold raffles or make presentations, so find out what is wanted. Make sure you know the finishing time, as an evening can end unhappily with an angry caretaker.

Try to plan your dances to suit the people present. Sometimes you have more girls (and occasionally more men), so have a few dances for two girls and one man (or vice versa) that you can do with them. Some dances are difficult at the beginning, as the early arrivals are often shy and reluctant to take to the floor. If necessary go down to the dance floor and bring people on. Most people want to dance but just don't want to be the first up. As soon as you've got started the problem usually disappears. Another difficulty is getting all the sets filled up quickly, so tell the incomplete ones to raise their hands so that other couples can join them.

Calling is not easy and there is a lot to learn. Apart from keeping everyone happy you have to teach and instruct without appearing to do so. To some people it can be very nerve-racking, so make certain you really want to do it. Go to lots of dances and see other Callers at work. Make a note of any good dances you have not seen before. If you have called dances for a few friends but want to call at big dances, try to find some musicians or a band that you can work with. It is much easier to work with people you know, and you can share the cost of an amplification system.

Amplification

Amplification is essential for the Caller, and most bands find it necessary too. A good public address system is expensive and you will need to get quite a few engagements to pay off the cost. A P.A. system consists of a mixer, amplifier, microphones and speakers. Some Callers and individual musicians have what is known as a "combo", which is a large speaker with a built-in amplifier – an all-in-one sound system. A Caller needs a microphone with a built-in on/off switch. A band can play in front of microphones on stands, or some instruments can be fitted with their own microphones. Electric guitars plug into their own amplifier direct. Acoustic guitars and violins can be fitted with a bug, and accordions or melodeons with an internal microphone. Sound equipment comes in varying sizes and varying power. 100 watts is quite powerful enough for any folk band, although Rock super groups belt out a lot more sound than this. Make sure you have a good-quality mixer, without which it is difficult to get the sound balance right. Some bands run a cable to the back of the hall and put the mixer there, with an operator to keep the sound balanced – very sophisticated but impractical for the small band.

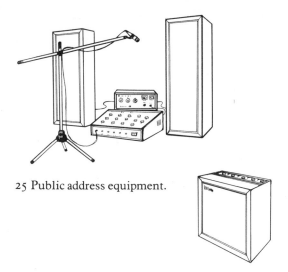

25 Public address equipment.

26 A "combo" speaker: with a built-in amplifier.

If you intend to play records to dance to in big halls you will need a P.A. with a record player attachment and a microphone to speak through.

Keep an eye open for second-hand equipment. Lots of young people buy amplifiers and speakers and then decide to sell them, so bargains can be found. Before deciding, it is best to take expert advice. A P.A. is expensive and you will probably want to use the equipment for a long time.

CHAPTER SEVEN

Playing together in a band

A good band must be good to dance to. You can strive to be musically interesting and original for your own enjoyment, but the dancers will be hardly aware of what you are doing as long as you provide a good background of music that makes them want to dance. In fact, they will sometimes only notice if the band is playing badly – sad but true!

The band can have any number of musicians. They can play any instruments, wear any clothes, they can stand up or sit down, they may be very old or quite young, but to be good their music has to have three ingredients: rhythm, timing and enthusiasm.

Rhythm is the basis of all dancing and although the traditional tunes seem simple and uncomplicated in form you must accent them with a very marked up-beat, whether you play a tin whistle, drum, accordion or fiddle. Some instruments, like the melodeon or anglo-concertina, have an inbuilt bouncy rhythm because of the pull-push action of the bellows. Others, like the fiddle, depend entirely on the musical talent of the player to give the melody that touch of lilt that is the essence of the music. The surest way to acquire it is to listen to other players whose style you admire. There are also many excellent recordings of traditional players both on records and tapes, and these are a marvellous source of inspiration. A list of some of the good ones is given on page 60. Some are superb musicians, some are not, but they all infuse their music with a drive and life that make it special and part of a continuing tradition.

Good timing comes with experience and knowledge of the dances. It helps if you enjoy dancing yourself. Find the right pace for the dancers, and then keep it steady right through the dance, only speeding up if that's what they want to do. If you are playing for beginners, and that's likely if you are a beginner yourself, emphasize the eight-bar phrases clearly. That will help them know when to expect the next change of figure. Give a good clear chord or two to start the dance, and make sure everyone in the band knows when to stop – not as easy as it seems.

Enthusiasm for the music may not necessarily manifest itself in a happy laughing band. Although it's nice if it does, some players may look rather serious when they are concentrating on their music. The important thing is for the band really to enjoy what they play and this will show in their music, immediately communicating a sense of jollification to the evening's dancing.

How to get the band started? Most bands start with a group of friends wanting to play together. It certainly helps if you like the people you team up with. You want to have broad agreement on the style and music you choose, and you all need to be prepared for many hours of getting together and practising. Sometimes members of a family start a band, and this can often prove a sure way of togetherness. The incredible Irish "McCuskers Band" was composed of a family of eight brothers.

If possible you want to aim at a good balance of sound. Have both rhythm and melody in the band, and some bass if you can get it.

Melody line	Fiddle, whistles or flute. Accordion, melodeon, concertina. (These are useful because they have rhythm accompaniment as well.)
Rhythm	Guitar, banjo, piano, drums, tambourine.
Bass line	Bass guitar, double bass, tuba, bassoon. (These are all bulky expensive instruments and a band starting up is lucky to have one of them.)

There are many other instruments you could use to give additional colour to the overall sound, and the following list shows the diversity of instruments used by some popular bands of the past and present. It also proves that the number of musicians is of little consequence, if the musical quality is good.

Accordion,	Melodeons,	Accordion,
Fiddle,	Concertina,	Guitar,
Double Bass,	Trombone,	Drums
Piano, Drums	Banjo, Washboard	

Fiddle,	Fiddle,	Melodeon, Banjo,
Concertina,	Accordion,	Hammered Dulcimer,
Banjo,	Saxophone,	Trombone, Piano,
Cello	Piano, Drums	Drums, Tuba

Melodeon,		Melodeon,
Concertina,		Tambourine
Electric Guitar, Drums,		
Electric Bass Guitar		

The first thing is to find the tunes you want to play. You will need to make selections of jigs, reels, marches, hornpipes and waltzes. Pick up good tunes whenever you can. Learn from other players, recordings or printed music, of which there is a considerable selection. There are lots of good books in print at the moment, but there is also good music to be had second-hand. If most of the band prefer to play initially from music, then write out as many copies as you need. Many musicians who play for dancing prefer to play from memory, as they can then watch the progression of the dancers and keep a closer co-ordination with the other players.

There are certain rules that the beginner playing for dancing needs to know. Most tunes are made up of two lines of music called A and B. Each line takes up one figure in the dance and is often repeated by both dancers and musicians. It is composed of eight bars of music and allows the dancers to take sixteen steps. If A and B music are both played twice through they make 32 bars, and this is the usual length for most dances. A few such as "The Bridge of Athlone" and "The Waves of Tory" require forty-eight bars, and for these it is best to choose a tune that contains a third eight-bar line, which you play twice. (See chapter five for more detail about the structure of dances.)

The phrasing of the tunes is important to the dancers, as it gives continuity to the movement. The note that leads into the music, the up-beat, is particularly important, as it sparks off the action. What musicians do by instinctive feeling is to divide an eight-bar line into two two-bar phrases balanced by a four-bar phrase. In the two-bar phrases the emphasis is at the beginning of the 2nd bar and the longer phrase leads back to a repeat of the melody: a combination of rise and fall and flow which makes the music danceable.

Some bands play a selection of two tunes that fit well together, others usually play a selection of three. If you feel that this is beyond you to begin with, then just play one good tune through the whole dance, perhaps with some instrumental variations.

Many dances have set tunes, and if this is the case it is usually best to use them. Add another one or two to make a medley if you like, but find tunes that have the same rhythm, because although it is nice to have changes of key it is easiest from the dancers' point of view to merge tunes that have exactly the same rhythm and balance. Some dances have a change of rhythm within the dance, from reel to jig for instance. This is great fun to play and adds interest to the music, but it can only be done with certain dances.

Choose music that is within the capabilities of all the musicians. Remember you have to keep going for three or four hours if you are playing for a dance, and that requires stamina. It takes time to build up a repertoire of tunes. Don't worry if you run out of music when the band is new and inexperienced. Just play a selection twice. The dancers will not mind – in fact, they may not even notice. When the Caller announces the dance it is a good idea for the band to strike up and play a tune once through just to encourage people to get up on the dance floor. You will also need to have some set pieces ready to play between dances when everyone is having a break. You are going to be doing a lot of playing for an evening's dancing, and with luck that should be a lot of fun.

CHAPTER EIGHT

Running a dance

Social and sports clubs, Parent-Teacher groups, scout troops and schools often run barn dances successfully, and you may decide to do the same. If it is to be a very small affair with friends dancing to your own music or records, all you need to do is find a suitable hall or large room and provide refreshments. If it is to be more ambitious, with an outside band and Caller booked, you will need to do something more. These things can carry quite a financial risk, so ask yourself before you start if you are prepared for the work, worry and time involved. It is best to try to get a group of people to share the organization. This not only reduces the financial liability but spreads the work load and helps increase the numbers at the dance, as all those involved will be committed to telling their friends about it.

Book your band, Caller and hall well in advance. Good bands are often booked months ahead, so leave plenty of time.

If you need a hall, try the local churches, schools, pubs and sports clubs. Libraries and local council offices usually provide lists of halls for hire. Decide if you want a bar. Most church halls and schools are not licensed and you can run into legal difficulties if you sell alcohol. If you want a bar and your dancers are over eighteen it is simplest to use licensed premises or ask a local publican to run the bar for you. Whatever you do, enquire about local licensing laws first. If you run a non-alcoholic dance you must still provide something to drink – dancing is hot work. Some groups serve food at barn dances, French bread and cheese and hot dogs all in the price of admission, and a glass of wine or beer may also be legally dispensed this way. This often adds a good atmosphere to the evening, and is worth the extra work.

THE BAND AND CALLER Try to book a band and Caller you have heard or have had recommended to you. If this is not possible get in touch with your nearest English Folk Dance and Song Society office for advice. (Addresses are listed on page 61.) The E.F.D.S.S. publish annually a folk directory listing bands, Callers etc. Local folk clubs and Morris sides might also give you advice, and you may find information in local papers. You can often book a band and Caller together. If you book them separately make sure that they can work together – square dance Callers like to work with music to suit them, and you can have problems. Ask your band about amplification. Most will provide it, but a few do not, so find out when you book. They will want to know:

The age group of the dancers, and their degree of experience.
The starting and finishing times of the dance.
The organizer's name and telephone number.
The address of the venue.
The size of the hall and the expected numbers.
The stage arrangements.

THE HALL Try to make the hall look attractive. Some school halls can look very bare and it is difficult to create a good atmosphere. Put up some decorations and dim the lights. Old-fashioned bunting always looks nice – the local scouts might lend you some. Branches of evergreen leaves can help to make the place look festive. Have your decorations in keeping with the evening. Leave the Wild West look to an American Square Dancing evening.

DRESS People will often ask what to wear for a barn dance. Country dancing is very energetic and you may get hot. Wear clothes that you can discard easily as the evening progresses, and comfortable shoes that you can move about quickly in. With these factors in mind you can be as formal or as informal as you like.

PUBLICITY Give your dance as much publicity as you possibly can. Think of every way to let people know you are having a dance. Posters are very important, so put them out well in advance. If you have to design them yourself but cannot do lettering use Letraset transfer. Photocopying is relatively cheap so you can reproduce your designs quickly and easily. You may be able to persuade the local newspaper to print information about the dance. Local radio is often helpful.

27 Country dancing at Berkshire Midsummer Folk Festival.

THE DANCE ITSELF Before the dance make a duty rota with all the other helpers. Nobody likes sitting at the door selling tickets all evening, so be fair and share the work out. Make things as easy as possible for the band and Caller when they arrive. Let them know of any raffles, presentations or entertainments so that they can plan the evening. Most bands and Callers appreciate the offer of a drink, and if you think they have given you a good evening tell them so. Make sure the Caller knows the right time to end the dance. Publicans, vicars and caretakers can get irritable if you over-run, so always finish with time for the dancers to have a chat before leaving and for the organizers to return the hall to normality.

28 Dancing at Cecil Sharp House.

In spite of all the worries of running a dance it's almost always worth it. Nothing is so satisfying as providing people with the chance to enjoy them-selves, and when you've achieved your first dance you will soon be looking forward to the next.

Useful information

Useful records to dance to

*KICKIN' UP THE SAWDUST Ashley Hutchins	EMI Records SHSP 4073
ENGLISH FOLK DANCES The Country Dance Band The Northumbrian Barnstormers McBains Band	EMI Records CLP 3754
ENGLISH FOLK DANCES Jimmy Shand and his Band	EMI Records OU 2015
*CHEVIOT BARN DANCE The Cheviot Ranters	Topic Records 12TS245
*THE CHEVIOT HILLS The Cheviot Ranters	Topic Records 12TS222
THE RAKES	Leader Sound LED 2071

*These records have dance instructions printed on the sleeve.

Records of traditional players

ENGLISH COUNTRY MUSIC	Topic Records 12T296
BOB CANN – WEST COUNTRY MELODEON	Topic Records 12TS275
THE ART OF WILLIAM KIMBER	Topic Records 12T249

Many of the best Folk dance records are produced on the Leader and Topic labels. We list a few from the many available. Catalogues from:
Topic Records, 27 Nassington Road, London NW3 2TX.
Leader Sound Ltd., 209 Rochdale Road, Halifax, West Yorkshire HX4 8JE.

A special recording by 'Old Mole' of the music for the ten dances in Chapter Five is available on Pan Records OM 793. Details from Pansound, 73 Ealing Park Gardens, London W5 4ET, or the Folk Shop, Cecil House, address next page.

Addresses

The English Folk Dance and Song Society,
Cecil Sharp House,
2 Regent's Park Road,
London NW1 7AY.
Tel: 01–485 2206

The Society publishes books and records on Folk Dance. It runs a Folk shop in London with an excellent postal service, issuing catalogues of all Folk Dance publications and records in print. It promotes dances and Folk Festivals and each year publishes the *Folk Directory*, which is an invaluable handbook of useful information and addresses of bands, Callers and dance clubs.

The regional E.F.D.S.S. addresses are:

MIDLAND REGION
75 Green Lane,
Kettering,
Northants NN1 5oDA.
Tel: 0536 83901.

NORTHERN REGION
5 Norfolk Mount,
Chapel Allerton,
Leeds LS7 4PU.
Tel: 0532 694764.

EASTERN REGION
High View,
Ashfield Green,
Wickhambrook,
Newmarket, Suffolk.
Tel: 044082 666

WESTERN REGION
Folk House,
10 Richmond Road,
Exeter,
Devon EX4 4JF.
Tel: 0392 77285/6

The area offices all publicize events, dances etc., of local interest.

The Performing Rights Society,
29/33 Berners Street,
London W1P 4AA.
Tel: 01–580 5544.

This Society publishes pamphlets of information relating to the laws of music copyright, and if you decide to take up calling or playing seriously you should familiarize yourself with this information. The E.F.D.S.S. has published its own pamphlet called *Copyright and The Law in Relation to Folk* and this explains the position of folk music performance in relatively simple terms.

Useful books of dances and music

The Community Dances Manuals 1–7,
E.F.D.S.S. publications.
Dances from the Yorkshire Dales, Leta Douglas,
E.F.D.S.S. publications.

Books of music

The Fiddler's Tune Book 1 and 2.
The Charlton Northumbrian Pipers Tune Book.
The Dorchester Hornpipe   Country dance tunes
from the family manuscript book of Thomas Hardy.
O'Neill's Collections of Tunes for Irish Music.
Kerr's Collections of Tunes for Scottish Music.

29 At the Sidmouth Folk Festival.

Folk Festivals

Folk Festivals provide a good chance for dancing to a variety of fine bands and Callers. They have workshops to help musicians, dancers and Callers. We list a few, but the E.F.D.S.S. will supply information on them all.

APRIL	Poynton, Cheshire.
MAY	Chippenham and Laycock
	Felixstowe.
JUNE	Berkshire.
JULY	Bracknell.
AUGUST	Broadstairs
	Sidmouth
	Whitby
	Towersey.
SEPTEMBER	Bromyard.

Index